Module 9: Assessments, Exams & R

Introduction

Undertaking assessments and preparing for examinations can be difficult and confusing. This module will help you to understand a range of assessment types and also act as a revision tool to help you prepare for examinations in any academic discipline. It will help you develop revision and memorisation techniques and also familiarise you with different exam question types and tasks.

Unit 1 analyses a range of assessments that you might be required to undertake. Unit 2 guides you through the revision planning stage, building on what you already know about exams and how to prepare for them. Unit 3 looks at effective study skills techniques and active learning strategies to help you when you study. Unit 4 deals with ways to revise and prepare for exams and suggests strategies that can be used. Unit 5 looks at some common pitfalls and problems. Steps to avoid exam-related stress are discussed in Unit 6.

At the end of this module, you will have developed a basic understanding of some common assessment formats. You will have also developed a more structured and tailored examination technique for individual study purposes. You will be more aware of what the exam questions are asking you to do and what to include in your answers.

Contents

Understanding assessment tasks

At the end of this unit, you will:

- understand how to answer essay questions
- be able to maximise your performance on multiple-choice questions

Task 1 Instruction words

1.1 Work individually. Match the instruction words with their explanation.

a.

| analyse | comment on | compare | contrast | define |

comment on Identify the main issues and give an informed opinion.

_____ Show how two things are different. Explain the consequences of dissimilarities.

_____ Examine in detail by dividing up. Identify the main points.

_____ Give the precise meaning of a term. This may include explaining what is problematic about defining the term.

_____ Show how two things are similar. Explain the consequences of the similarities.

b.

| describe | discuss | evaluate | examine | explain |

_____ Look at the most important aspects of something in a balanced way, i.e., advantages and disadvantages, for and against.

_____ Give the main features, characteristics or events.

_____ Assess how important or useful something is. It is likely to include both positive and negative points.

_____ Provide reasons for why something happens, or why something is in a particular state.

_____ Take a detailed look at something.

c.

| illustrate | interpret | justify | outline | make a case |

_____ Put forward an argument either for or against a claim.

_____ Give the meaning or significance of something.

_____ Give the main ideas or information, without any details.

_____ Show what something is like, using examples and/or evidence.

_____ Support a claim with evidence, but taking into account opposing views.

d.

| relate | state | summarise | to what extent | trace |

_____ Put the steps and stages of a process or event into order.

_____ Give the main points only, using fewer words than the original.

_____ Give the connections between things.

_____ Say how much something is or isn't true.

_____ Give just the main points, very clearly.

1.2 Work with a partner to compare your answers, then discuss any differences of opinion.

1.3 How does the change in instruction word change each task?

a. *Trace* the events which led to the French Revolution.

b. *Interpret* the significance of the French Revolution for contemporary France.

c. *Analyse* the impact of the French Revolution on nineteenth-century Europe.

1.4 Work with a partner to discuss which instruction words are most common in your academic area.

Task 2 Question styles

2.1 If possible, work with another student who studies the same course as you. Answer the questions.

a. Will you need to answer essay questions? If so, how many?

b. Which types of essay might you expect to have?

c. Will you have multiple-choice questions?

d. Which other question types are you likely to have?

e. Do any of your subjects require calculations to be shown? Why is it important to show this if it is required?

Task 3 Exam essay planning and title analysis

3.1 Read the essay title and break it down into smaller parts by asking yourself questions relating to the different sections.

> Studying the English language in an English-speaking country is the best way to learn the language. It is not possible to learn the language properly without spending time living in an anglophone environment. Discuss.

a. How many parts is the essay title made up of?

b. Which issues need to be discussed in part 1?

c. Which issues need to be discussed in part 2?

d. What is the overall task you are expected to do?

   1. Put a process in order.

   2. Show what an English-speaking country is like, giving examples.

   3. Look at the question in a balanced way.

   4. Give a one-word answer.

3.2 Now write a short plan for the essay.

On page 29 you will find a model of how Task 3.1 *could* be completed. Do not look at this model until you have completed Task 3.2.

1

Task 4 Planning and analysis in practice

4.1 Choose one of the essays below and repeat the steps suggested in Task 3.1. Try to spend no more than 5–10 minutes on this exercise.

Essay titles:

a. Secondary schools should redesign the curriculum in order to concentrate solely on teaching children the academic disciplines that are required for employment. It is a waste of time to devote school-time to subjects such as Art and General Studies. Discuss.

b. Examination is the only way to judge students' abilities. Institutions insist that, without examination, it is difficult to judge a student's proficiency in any field.
Do you agree or disagree? Give reasons to support your answer.

Task 5 Identifying examination skills

5.1 Consider the different types of questions you might need to answer in an exam. What do you need to be able to do in an exam? Make a list in the 'type of question' column of the table.

5.2 Next, complete the table by identifying which skills you will need to be able to answer each question properly.

type of question	skills practice required
Answering questions based on a text	• understanding questions fully
	• skimming and scanning
Essay writing	• essay planning
	• title analysis

Task 6 Timed essay writing

6.1 Practise writing one of the essays from Task 4.
  - Use your plan.
  - Set a time limit.
  - For further guidance on academic writing, consult the *Essay Writing* and *Scientific Writing* modules from the TASK series.

Task 7 Answering multiple-choice questions

7.1 Select a series of multiple-choice questions from a past paper and follow the four steps indicated below.

Step 1

Read all the questions for the first time and write a * next to those questions that you think you are able to answer easily. Write ? next to those questions that you are not sure about. Lastly, write ! alongside any questions that you really do not know the answer to.

Step 2

Answer all the questions that you have marked *. This should be the quickest section to complete, as you are fairly certain that you know the answers.

Step 3

Now that you have had some time to think about the questions in front of you and you have completed the most straightforward items, answer the questions which have been marked ?. These are the questions that you need to think more carefully about. This section will probably take a little longer than the questions in Step 2.

Step 4

The remaining questions (which have been marked !), are the questions that you find the most difficult. In some multiple-choice examinations, you will lose marks if you give a wrong answer. This is called *negative marking*. If this system of marking is being used in your examination, you should avoid giving an answer that you are not sure of.
But if negative marking is not used, you should always attempt to give an answer, even if you are not sure that it is correct. However, don't spend a great deal of time on the questions that you don't know the answer to. You can return to these questions at the end of the exam if there is any time remaining.

1

Task 8 Short answer questions

8.1 Many exams include short answer questions that often ask you to define or explain a key term or concept. Read the paragraph and identify:

a. an example ____

b. an explanation ____

c. a definition ____

d. a topic sentence ____

[1]A monopoly is a very different form of market structure than perfect competition.

[2]A pure monopoly is when one firm has control of 100% of that market. [3]For instance, many nationalized industries control one particular sector such as health or electricity. [4]In a monopoly, there is a lack of choice for the consumer and the power is with the supplier.

8.2 Choose a term from an academic area you are studying. Write a definition of the term, including a topic sentence, an example and an explanation.

Reflect

Find a past exam from one of your subjects. What question types are there? What are the key instruction words in the essay questions?

2 Study skills and active learning

At the end of this unit, you will:

- understand various study skills strategies
- learn about strategies that help you to memorise information

Task 1 Study skills

1.1 Read about three study skills techniques. Work with a partner to rank them in order of the most effective to the least effective.

☐ **Highlighting**

Underlining or highlighting information in a text. Marked text draws the reader's attention, but additional processing is necessary if the reader has to decide which material is most important. Such decisions require the reader to think about the meaning of the text and how its different pieces relate to one another.

☐ **Self-explanation**

Involves an aspect of explaining the process during learning. The questions can be generic, e.g., *Explain what the sentence means to you.* That is, *what new information does the sentence provide for you? How does it relate to what you already know?* OR the question can be very specific to a context, e.g., *Why is the numerator 14 and the denominator 7 in this step?*

☐ **Practice testing**

Interpreted in its widest sense to include things such as recall of target information via the use of flashcards, completing practice problems or questions included at the end of textbook chapters, or completing practice tests included in the electronic supplementary materials that increasingly accompany textbooks.

1.2 Work with another pair and give reasons for your order.

1.3 Read the text. Discuss the questions with a partner.

    a.   Why do you think rereading is such a popular study strategy?

    b.   How effective do you think it is for helping you to remember information?

    c.   Practice testing and distributed practice (spreading your studies over a long period of time) are shown to be two of the most effective techniques for learning. Why do you think this is?

Rereading

This technique is commonly used by students. Carrier (2003) surveyed college students in an upper-division Psychology course and 65% reported using rereading as a technique when preparing for exams. Kornell and Bjork (2007) and Hartwig and Dunlosky (2012) found 18% of students reported rereading entire chapters, and 62% reported rereading parts or sections of the material. Karpicke et al. (2009) asked students to list all of the techniques used when studying and then to rank them in terms of frequency of use. Eighty-four per cent of students included rereading textbook/notes in their list – rereading was the top-ranked technique.

1.4 Read the texts. Complete the sentences using the words in the box.

elaborative interrogation	interleaved practice

Commonly, students block-study a topic from a subject. For example, content from one subtopic is studied or all problems of one type are practised before the student moves on to the next set of material. In contrast, a_____ is where students alternate practice between topics or problems.

The key to b_____ involves prompting learners to generate an explanation for an explicitly stated fact. This technique typically involves asking students to answer 'Why' questions, e.g., *Why does it make sense that …?, Why is this true?, Why would this fact be true of this [X] and not some other [X]?* and simply *Why?*. To a certain extent, this is akin to critical thinking.

1.5 Work with a partner to discuss the questions.

a. Have you ever used the techniques in Task 1.4?

b. Both techniques have been shown to help understanding and recall. Why do you think this is?

c. Think about the assessments you have to do soon. How could these techniques help you?

Task 2 A deeper understanding

Understanding information and ideas is important to both learning and remembering. To do this, it is useful to link ideas together into a framework or map. This map of ideas helps us to understand smaller pieces of information. It also helps us to remember them by linking them together into a meaningful whole. For example, it is easier to remember irregular verbs when we group them together. All academic subjects have core concepts. These are what help us make the framework or map.

2.1 **Study the parts of an object. Put them together to make a two-dimensional view of the whole object. What is the object?**

To make the object, you identified the different parts and organised them to make an understandable whole. This is also true of concepts.

2.2 **Read the definition of *society*. Break it down into its smaller parts by completing the table.**

'Society can be defined as a group of people who live in a particular place and tend to share a distinctive culture and set of institutions.'

concept	parts
society	

Task 3 Organising information into groups

3.1 **Read through the list of words in the box once. Close your book and write down as many as you can remember.**

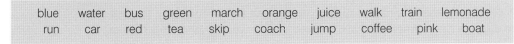

blue	water	bus	green	march	orange	juice	walk	train	lemonade
run	car	red	tea	skip	coach	jump	coffee	pink	boat

3.2 **Now try to write the words again. This time, use the categories: *colours*, *drinks*, *ways of moving* and *transport*.**

3.3 **Work with a partner to discuss the questions.**

a.   Did you remember more words the second time?

b.   If so, why?

2

Task 4 Reorganising information into diagrams

4.1 Match the descriptions (a–c) to the types of diagram (1–3).

a. Although this is less structured than a concept map, it also focuses on links between ideas. The key concept is in the centre of the map. Thick lines are connected to this centre and the thinner lines branch off these. Next to each line is a keyword. ☐

b. This is a diagram which is often used to show a process. It usually includes a starting point, an end point and a set of questions which require a decision. ☐

c. This type of diagram is used to put information in time order. ☐

1.

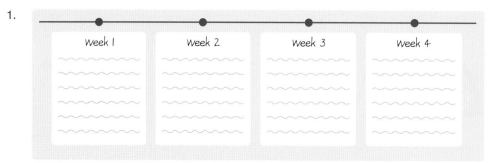

2.

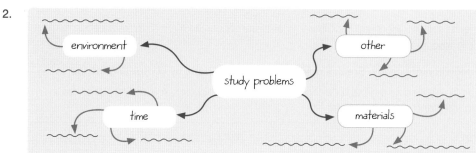

3.

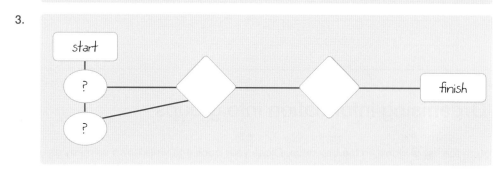

4.2 Choose a set of notes that you have taken on your subject area. Reorganise the notes into one of the diagram types. When you have finished, explain your diagram to a partner.

Task 5 Reorganising information into summary notes

5.1 Choose a different part of your notes. Read through the section carefully and divide the information into three levels: *thesis statement or most general claim*, *more specific claims* and *supporting points or evidence*. Rewrite the notes as a summary, using a different colour pen for each level of information.

5.2 Teach the information in your notes to a partner.

Reflect

Reflect on the understanding you have gained about your learning style. How do you think you can adapt the techniques in this unit to maximise your own learning?

At the end of this unit, you will:

- develop a good understanding of your examinations' requirements
- create a revision plan

Task 1 The purpose of examinations

1.1 Work with a partner to discuss the questions.

   a. Have you taken a written examination before?

   b. If so, how did you prepare for the examination?

   c. How did you feel a month before the examination?

   d. How did you feel on the day of the examination?

1.2 Work in small groups to discuss the questions.

   a. What is the purpose of examinations?

   b. What are the advantages of examinations?

Task 2 Examination requirements

2.1 Work with a partner to discuss all the possible sources of information about examination requirements, then complete the list.

   a. *student handbook*

   b. _____

   c. _____

   d. _____

2.2 Work individually. Consider each module/subject for which you will have an examination and complete a table similar to the one below for each exam.

module/subject title: _____		
exam location and timing	exam structure and organisation	topics

2.3 Compare your table with another student who is sitting an examination in the same module/subject.

Task 3 Planning for an exam

3.1 When you have completed Task 2, ask your subject tutors to help you complete the sections in the Exam Planner below for each exam. This will help you to get organised in advance of the big day.

Exam Planner	module/subject		
date of examination			
location of examination (e.g., campus, building, room)			
items required (e.g., a form of identification)			
materials permitted for use in examination			
contribution of examination to final grade			
date of revision classes			
number of papers in examination			
recommended time allocation for each section of examination			
types of question in each of the different question papers			
subject areas covered in examination			
recommended books and further reading			

3

Task 4 Revision timetable

4.1 Using the information from the Exam Planner you completed in Task 3, complete this Study Planner with a module/subject in each box. Make a note of the time you spend revising. Plan to start revising at least four weeks before the day of your first examination.

Study Planner	Monday		Tuesday		Wednesday	
	a.m.	p.m.	a.m.	p.m.	a.m.	p.m.
Week 1						
	a.m.	p.m.	a.m.	p.m.	a.m.	p.m.
Week 2						
	a.m.	p.m.	a.m.	p.m.	a.m.	p.m.
Week 3						
	a.m.	p.m.	a.m.	p.m.	a.m.	p.m.
Week 4						
	a.m.	p.m.	a.m.	p.m.	a.m.	p.m.
Week 5						
	a.m.	p.m.	a.m.	p.m.	a.m.	p.m.
Week 6						

Date and time of examinations:

Thursday		Friday		Saturday		Sunday	
a.m.	p.m.	a.m.	p.m.	a.m.	p.m.	a.m.	p.m.
a.m.	p.m.	a.m.	p.m.	a.m.	p.m.	a.m.	p.m.
a.m.	p.m.	a.m.	p.m.	a.m.	p.m.	a.m.	p.m.
a.m.	p.m.	a.m.	p.m.	a.m.	p.m.	a.m.	p.m.
a.m.	p.m.	a.m.	p.m.	a.m.	p.m.	a.m.	p.m.
a.m.	p.m.	a.m.	p.m.	a.m.	p.m.	a.m.	p.m.

3

Task 5 Revision timetable

5.1 It is important to spend some time relaxing during your revision period. Too much revision without incentives or free-time activities can lead to boredom and lack of concentration. Take another look at your Study Planner and add at least two fun activities for each week. Focusing on your studies may be easier if you have a few enjoyable activities to look forward to in the near future.

Reflect

Now you have completed your Study Planner, reflect on what you have done. Are you sure you have the right balance? For example, think about when you are most focused – at what time of day do you find it easiest to study? Spend time reflecting on all the relevant issues before making any changes to your Study Planner.

4 Revision strategies

At the end of this unit, you will:

- be aware of the benefits of active revision
- have a personal revision strategies toolkit

Task 1 Pass or fail

1.1 Make a list of reasons why a student might pass or fail an exam. Then work in small groups to compare your answers.

pass	fail

1.2 Think about an exam in which you did well. What helped you to do well? Work with a partner to discuss your answers.

Task 2 Active and passive revision

The best revision advice is to revise actively. Active revision helps you develop a bigger picture of the subject area. You should aim to develop your understanding and link any new ideas to what you already confidently understand.

2.1 Read the letter. What advice would you give this student to help improve her active revision?

Dear Study Doc,

I really need some help with my revision. In preparation for my end-of-year exams, I went to the library every day. I just don't know why I didn't get the grades I was expecting.

Nearly every day, I arranged to sit with Zahra, one of the really brainy girls from my Economics class. She seemed to follow a really strict study schedule. I watched her studying and she wrote the most detailed notes. She was really focused on what she was doing. I could even see which subject she was studying by the colour of her folder!

I remember that the view from my desk overlooked the playing fields and I could see a different sport every day, both in the morning and in the afternoon.

That really helped me to relax. On average I was in that library for about seven hours every day. I work better in the mornings, so I tried to make myself study for at least three hours without a break. Then, in the afternoon, I gave myself a short break every 15 minutes.

I really don't know how Zahra managed to study so hard and take such great care of her appearance. She wore a different outfit every day. I used to try and guess what she would be wearing before she arrived.

Although I spent more than ten consecutive days in the library before my exams, I didn't find the exam paper easy at all. The day before my Economics paper, I spent a whole day trying to understand our textbook, but even though I read the same passages over and over again, the ideas never really stuck in my head. I read and reread the same pages, but I seemed to get more and more confused.

What do you think I'm doing wrong? I'd appreciate your advice.

Olena Govorovska
(Undergraduate: Business and Economics)

2.2 Work in small groups to discuss your advice and make a note of any points that you hadn't thought of.

2.3 Write your reply.

Task 3 Reading past papers

It is possible that your tutor will be able to provide you with past examination papers that have been used for assessment in previous years. Alternatively, they may be available in the university library or on the home page of your university department.

3.1 Why do you think it might be useful to look at past papers? Discuss your ideas with a partner.

3.2 Once you have got a copy of a past paper, use the four stages below to help you to learn from it.

Stage 1 Choose a question from one section in your past paper and calculate the amount of time which is realistically available to answer the question. Base your answer on the overall exam time and the recommended time allocation for each part of the exam.

Stage 2 Build into your time limit some time to read the question thoroughly and plan your answer. In your plan, you will need to consider the following elements:
* key points to include
* how the question relates to the syllabus
* how the answer could be structured
* examples and evidence

Stage 3 Having decided on the amount of time you need to plan and answer the question, write your answer within the time.

Stage 4 After completing your answer, compare it with your notes and check for accuracy. Monitor the time you have used and ensure that your schedule is realistic.

Task 4 Revision toolkit

4.1 Students rely on a range of different revision tools according to their academic discipline and their learning style. Think back to what you learned in Unit 2. Then look at the list of revision strategies below and select at least five which you feel could realistically assist you in your revision.

- Check your understanding by comparing your notes with published material. ☐
- Make sure that your notes are complete. Refer to lecture outlines and any recommended reading. ☐
- Summarise your notes by identifying key theories and information. ☐
- Make summaries of your notes in diagrammatic form. ☐
- Produce index cards with key facts and data in an easy-to-remember format. ☐
- Think and make a note of connections between different topics to see how subjects interrelate. You can draw mind maps for this. ☐
- Adapt a series of data for use in a table or a graph. ☐
- Familiarise yourself with past papers and question formats. ☐
- Practise identifying key elements in the question rubric. ☐
- Consider different ways of answering a question and evaluate them. ☐
- Meet with other students to discuss and compare your understanding of different topics and to identify gaps in your knowledge. ☐
- Schedule meetings with your tutor to monitor your revision progress. ☐
- Use over-learning: rewrite information from notes and read it often. Do this for a short amount of time, but over several days. ☐
- _____
- _____
- _____
- _____
- _____

4.2 Add any missing strategies to the list above.

Reflect

After looking at some past papers, think about the kind of exam questions you would write for each of the key areas in your own area of study. This will help you to develop a deeper understanding of the exam style and a better approach to revision.

At the end of this unit, you will:

- understand how the question paper is organised
- be able to follow instructions on question papers more accurately

Task 1 The question paper cover

1.1 Study the cover of the question paper and identify the key information and important points to remember.

◆◇◆ The University of Lonbridge

Do not write anything until the invigilator informs
you that you may start the examination.

You will be given time at the end of the examination
to complete the front of any answer books used.

Candidate Number: ☐☐☐☐☐☐☐☐☐☐

1 Question Book
1 Answer Book
Dictionaries are not permitted

English Skills

Two hours and thirty minutes

Write your answers in the Answer Book provided

Section A Listening	20 marks	Section B Reading	20 marks	Section C Writing	40 marks	Section D Grammar	20 marks
	30 mins		30 mins		1 hour		30 mins

Each section will be weighted to contribute 25% towards the total score.

Task 2 The rubric

2.1 Read the examples of rubrics from question papers and answer the questions with a partner.

   a. What are the most important items of information?

   b. What types of mistakes do you think candidates are likely to make?

> Answer a total of three questions: two questions from Section A and one question from Section B.

> **Answer any ten of the following questions:**

> Candidates should answer five complete questions only.

> **Answer all of Part A, two questions from Part B and one question from Part C.**

Task 3 Following instructions

3.1 Complete the tasks given in the exam paper as you would under exam conditions – this means you cannot speak. Complete the tasks as fast as possible. Put up your hand when you have finished.

> **Please follow the instructions below carefully.**
>
> **Read through all the instructions before starting the tasks.**
>
> Use your answer sheet where necessary.
>
> 1. Write your name in the top left-hand corner of the answer sheet.
> 2. Underneath, write your birthday, favourite colour and favourite food.
> 3. Draw a box around this information and pass the answer sheet to the person on your right.
> 4. On the new answer sheet you have received, write your name in the middle of the sheet and your date of birth, eye colour and shoe size underneath. Draw a box around this information and pass the answer sheet to your right.
> 5. At the bottom of the new answer sheet, write a sentence comparing the information about the two people.
> 6. Pass the answer sheet to the right again. Read the sentence and underline the most interesting information.
> 7. Add another sentence, explaining why you believe the part you underlined is the most interesting information.
> 8. Pass the answer sheet to the right. Read the sentences on your new answer sheet. Decide whether you agree with the opinion or not and write a sentence explaining your opinion.
> 9. Return the answer sheet to the person whose name is in the top left-hand corner.
> 10. Ignore instructions 1–9. Close your books.

3.2 Read the instructions given in the question paper and the completed answer sheet on the next page. What mistakes has the candidate made? Work individually and then compare answers with a partner.

> The candidate should answer one question from Section A and all questions from Sections B and C. Answers should be transferred onto the answer sheet before the end of the exam.
>
> ## Section A Questions 1–3
>
> **Circle the correct answer.**
>
> 1. Which one of the following descriptions best explains the term 'membrane'?
>   a. the liquid in an animal cell
>   b. what gives plant cells their shape
>   c. the liquid-filled space in a plant cell
>   d. the thin outer layer of an animal cell
>
> 2. Which organ in the picture is the kidney?
>
>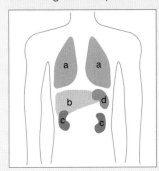
>
> 3. Which two of the following statements are true?
>   a. When cells divide, two identical cells are formed.
>   b. Cell division is necessary for growth.
>   c. A cell must have a nucleus in order to divide.
>   d. A cell must have a wall in order to grow.
>
> ## Section B Questions 4–6
>
> **Complete the description of respiration. Write no more than one word for each answer.**
>
> Respiration may be defined as the process of **4.** _____ energy from food. The analogy of burning fuel is often used to describe the process. Here the fuel is **5.** _____.
>
> For this, **6.** _____ is the key molecule. In plants, this is produced through photosynthesis.
>
> ## Section C Questions 7–10
>
> **Complete the following equation for respiration, using chemical symbols.**
>
> **7.** _____ $+ O_2 =$ **8.** _____ $+$ **9.** _____ $+$ energy
>
> **10.** What is the full name of the special energy-rich molecule in which the energy is stored?
>
> _____

5

Answer sheet
1. the thin outer layer of an animal cell
2. b, c
3. a
4. releasing some
5. glucose
6.
7. Glucose
8. Carbon dioxide
9. Water
10. ATP

Reflect

Think about the type of mistakes you have made when taking examinations in the past. How could you avoid these mistakes next time? Spend time thinking about what you have learned in this unit and how it can have an effect on your future results.

6 Managing exam stress

At the end of this unit, you will:

- understand how to manage anxiety while you are revising
- create a plan for managing your stress on the day of the exam

Task 1 Begin to take control

One important aspect of coping with exam stress is staying in control. People often feel stressed if they are unable to manage or control a situation. Obviously, you can't control the content of your exams, but you can take control of the examination situation in other ways.

1.1 **Work with a partner to discuss the ways in which you could take control of your revision and the preparation for your exams, based on what you have covered so far in this module.**

Task 2 Taking a positive attitude

2.1 **Read the advice. Then work with a partner to add two more pieces of advice.**

a. Make time in your revision schedule to relax. Find the best time of day and the best way to do this: take an exercise class, sing in the shower, listen to music.

b. Try to picture yourself arriving for the exam feeling happy and confident. Imagine this in as much detail as possible. This can help you replace any negative thoughts with more positive ones.

c. Avoid last-minute panic. Try not to revise up until the minute before the exam starts.

- _____

- _____

2.2 **Work with a partner to discuss which ideas would work best for you.**

Task 3 Managing your anxiety

3.1   Read through some ways of managing your anxiety in the examination. Match the headings (a–e) with the techniques (1–5).

a.   Paying attention to detail
b.   Breathe
c.   Think positive
d.   Stop!
e.   A calming presence

1.   Think of a person or a place you have positive associations with. Bring or wear an object to the exam which reminds you of this person or place. Touch it when you need to calm down.

2.   Replace negative thoughts such as 'I'm totally useless at this' and 'I just can't do this' with more positive ones: 'I am feeling stressed, but this exam won't kill me' and 'This isn't as bad as I thought it might be'.

3.   To stop yourself having negative thoughts, listen to yourself shout 'STOP!' in your head, or imagine a STOP road sign.

4.   Distract yourself from negative thoughts by listening hard for a few moments. Pay attention to all the sounds you can hear.

5.   When you feel anxious, your breathing changes, which can make you feel even more stressed! Try breathing deeply. This can help you stay calm and positive.

Task 4 Action points

4.1 The following recommendations have been identified as key to the management of exam stress. Read the bullet points and consider how you might put each recommendation into action.

- Get in control.

a. _I would make sure that I have allowed enough time for sufficient revision._

- Ensure you are both mentally and physically prepared.

b. I would _____

- Make sure you have the necessary equipment.

c. I would _____

- Make sure that you know what the format of the examination will be and what the marking system is.

d. I would _____

- Tackle your weak areas of understanding well in advance.

e. I would _____

- Think positively.

f. I would _____

- Discuss your concerns.

g. I would _____

Reflect

Think about stressful times you have experienced. Has the stress always been negative, or has it sometimes added something to your life? You will probably find when looking back that there has been a positive aspect.

Reflect on the positive aspects of stress and think about how you can harness this for exam preparation.

Web work

Website 1

Exam preparation

http://www.uea.ac.uk/services/students/let/study_resources/revision_exams/revision_faqs

Review

This online document gives advice on preparing for exams.

Task

Read the questions and decide which advice you think is the most helpful and why.

Website 2

Learner styles

http://www.learning-styles-online.com/inventory/

Review

This website provides a free online learning styles quiz. It represents your results graphically.

Task

Go online and take the test. Read about different learner styles in more detail and then use the information to plan your revision strategies.

Website 3

Managing exam stress

http://www.nottingham.ac.uk/currentstudents/healthyu/managing-exam-stress.aspx

Review

This website provides a guide for coping with exam stress.

Task

Print out the booklet and use a highlighter pen to mark the advice which you feel you could realistically apply.

Extension activities

Activity 1

Prepare a 'To Do' list for each of your exams and summarise the key areas which you will need to revise before the beginning of your exam period. As your revision progresses, you will be able to tick off the subjects that you have already covered and be able to view at a glance the areas which remain.

When you have compiled your 'To Do' list, have it checked by your tutor to make sure you haven't left anything out.

Activity 2

Complete a mock exam under timed exam conditions. This will give you experience of writing within a limited time frame. Ask a friend or a tutor to time you to make sure that you keep to the time limit. Practise any question types that you find difficult to complete under pressure.

Model answer

Unit 1 Task 3.1

Studying the English language in an English-speaking country is the best way to learn the language. It is not possible to learn the language properly without spending time living in an anglophone environment. Discuss.

Part 1
- Is studying the English language in an English-speaking country the best way to learn the language?
- Are there any other ways of learning a language effectively?

Part 2
- Is it true that it is not possible to learn the English language without spending time living in an anglophone environment?

Essay plan
- Introduction, including definition of key terms and a thesis statement. (Use James and Miller quote.)
- Explain the advantages of studying in the home culture in order to learn basic grammar. (Use cautious language, e.g., *One advantage may be …*)
- (Signposting, e.g., *On the other hand,*) Describe the advantages of studying in an anglophone environment in order to practise listening and speaking. (Use cautious language.)
- (Signposting, e.g., *To conclude*) Conclude that learning the basic grammar may be more effective in the home culture and that developing listening and speaking skills is often more successful in an English-speaking country.

G

Glossary

analyse (v) To break an issue down into parts in order to study, identify and discuss their meaning and/or relevance.

auditory learner (n) A learner who responds to sound when learning or recalling information. For example, an auditory learner may find it useful to memorise language through rhythmic repetition, may like to receive information aurally, and remember sounds, tunes and rhythms.

candidate (n) Someone who takes an exam, or is involved in another activity where selection and/or testing is involved, such as an application for an award or a job.

claim (n) (v) 1 (n) Something that is stated as true by a person or group, but is not universally accepted as a fact. 2 (v) To make a statement that you may believe to be true, but that is not universally accepted as such.

concept (n) The characteristics or ideas associated with a class or group of objects. For example, the concept 'city' brings to mind traits common to all places classed as 'cities'. 'Paris' is not a concept as it refers to a single, specific place.

concept map (n) A way of organising ideas that is similar to a mind map, but is more structured. It links a key general concept to more specific ideas with arrows.

contrast (n) (v) 1 (n) The differences that are evident between two things. 2 (v) To compare two or more things and identify differences between them and any consequences of their dissimilarities.

data (n) A collection of raw facts, such as statistics and figures. These need to be studied and interpreted in order to reach conclusions.

define (v) To give the precise meaning of a term or idea.

evaluate (v) To assess information in terms of quality, relevance, objectivity and accuracy.

evidence (n) Information and data that establish whether something is true or not.

flow chart (n) A diagram that shows a process. Steps or ideas are shown in a structured way (for example, from left to right or from top to bottom) and linked by arrows.

format (n) (v) 1 (n) The material presentation of information. The information to be revised can be put into several different formats, for example, in note form, as keywords and sentences on index cards, or visually, as a concept map. 2 (v) To apply a consistent style of presentation to information or data.

grade (n) (v) 1 (n) A mark for an essay, an exam or for overall performance on a course. Grades often correspond to a number, letter or word, such as 70%; 'A', 'C+' or 'F'; or Pass/Fail. 2 (v) To assess an essay, exam or overall performance and assign a grade.

interpret (v) Give the meaning or explain the significance of something as you understand it.

justify (v) Put forward a case for or against a knowledge claim or idea.

kinaesthetic learner (n) A learner who responds to movement and imitation when learning or recalling information. For example, a kinaesthetic learner may find it useful to memorise language by copying it out, and often takes extensive notes, draws pictures (doodles) or moves his/her hands and feet (fidgets) when memorising new information.

learning style (n) A style of thinking about, processing and remembering information that you have to learn. Different styles can be classified in a variety of ways. For example, you may have an auditory or kinaesthetic learning style.

memorisation (n) The process of learning 'by heart' or committing to memory.

mind map (n) A visual representation of ideas that are connected to each other. A key idea is written in the centre of the page and related ideas are written around it and connected by arrows (without too much deliberation). Mind mapping can be done in a group or individually to stimulate memory and/or organise thoughts.

multiple-choice (adj) Describes a question or task where students are given a set of several possible answers, normally only one of which is correct. They are required to choose the correct answer.

negative marking (n) A marking system (usually in an exam) where marks are deducted for incorrect answers.

outline (n) (v) 1 (n) A rough, often point-form sketch of the main ideas in a text or presentation. 2 (v) To give or make a rough sketch of the main ideas or events in a text or presentation.

over-learning (n) The process of going over information several times, even when you think you have learnt it. It may include rewriting of notes, rereading of texts, etc.

past paper (n) An examination paper from a previous exam. Past papers are often released for students to practise answering exam questions. They may be used in class or obtained for self-study.

relate (v) To show the connections between two or more things.

rubric (n) Written instructions for procedures and tasks on a test or exam paper or in a course book or handout.

scan (v) To look through a text quickly and pick out specific information.

schedule (n) (v) 1 (n) A plan that specifies the steps to take to complete a project and gives a clear time frame and/or deadlines for each part. 2 (v) To make a plan for how and when to complete a project.

skim (v) Read quickly through a text in order to get the gist or main idea.

strategy (n) A plan of action that you follow when you want to achieve a particular goal. For example, it is possible to have a clear strategy for passing an exam.

study aid (n) A device, system or support mechanism that makes study easier or helps you organise your study. For example, electronic organiser, study handbook, highlighter pen, etc.

summarise (v) To write or give a brief account of the main points of a text, lecture or idea.

supporting evidence (n) Information from academic sources that should be included in a piece of academic writing. This evidence illustrates and backs up your ideas and adds credibility to your work.

syllabus (n) A statement, outline or list of all the topics, skills and/or structures that will be covered in a course of study.

technique (n) A method or way of doing something that involves skill and/or efficiency. For example, it is possible to learn useful techniques for answering exam questions.

thesis statement (n) A statement that explains the controlling idea or main argument in a piece of academic writing. It is stated in the introduction and supported by reasons in the body of the essay.

time allocation (n) The time permitted or set aside to do something. For example, in an exam, some time may be allocated to read through the exam questions.

timeline (n) A visual representation of a set of events in a specified period that are shown on a line in the order that they happened.

title analysis (n) To break down an essay title into parts so that you can decide what type of essay it is, what to include in it and how to order your ideas.

toolkit (n) In academic life, this is a collection of resources, techniques or aids that help you to do something, for example, prepare for an exam.

trace (v) Put the steps and stages of a process or event into the correct order.

visual learner (n) A learner who responds to things they can see when learning or recalling information. For example, a visual learner often makes notes that are well laid-out, may highlight information using colour and likes to have handouts, OHTs and clear diagrams in a lecture.

Published by
Garnet Publishing Ltd
8 Southern Court
South Street
Reading RG1 4QS, UK

ISBN 978 1 78260 184 5

British Library Cataloguing-in-Publication Data

A catalogue record for this book is available from the British Library.

Production
Project Manager: Clare Chandler
Editorial team: Clare Chandler, Sophia Hopton,
                       Kate Kemp
Design & Layout: Madeleine Maddock
Photography: iStockphoto, Shutterstock

Garnet Publishing and the authors of TASK would like to thank the staff and students of the International Foundation Programme at the University of Reading for their respective roles in the development of these teaching materials.

Garnet Publishing would like to thank Jane Brooks for her contribution to the First edition of the TASK series.

All website URLs provided in this publication were correct at the time of printing. If any URL does not work, please contact your tutor, who will help you find similar resources.

Printed and bound in Lebanon by International Press:
interpress@int-press.com

Acknowledgements
Page 7:   Task 1.3, Rereading extract, taken from *Improving Students' Learning With Effective Learning Techniques: Promising Directions From Cognitive and Educational Psychology*, reproduced with kind permission of Sage Publishers.